The Bad Luck of KING FRED

CONTENTS

CHAPTER 1

King Frederick von Applegate III was very superstitious. He would never open an umbrella inside the palace, and everywhere he went, he carried with him a horseshoe, two four-leaf clovers, and his lucky penny. He would never walk under a ladder or get up on the wrong side of the bed. And he never ever could hear anybody sneeze without saying "gesundheit."

One day the king was sitting up in bed, enjoying his porridge. As he reached for his spoon, his new royal advisor burst through the door, causing the king's hand to jerk and knock over the salt shaker.

"Oh no, Your Majesty! It's terribly bad luck to spill salt. You must throw some over your left shoulder if you are to avoid total ruin," cried the advisor.

King Fred quickly did as the advisor cautioned, but he worried whether he had been fast enough to avoid the cloud of doom. "There's nothing harder to get rid of than bad luck once you've got it," King Fred mourned.

He thought a bit then said, "Make a royal proclamation that from now on all salt is banished from the kingdom. That will protect my subjects from the danger of spilling it."

Hear Ye! Hear Ye!

Let it be known that from this day forward, salt is banished from the kingdom by Royal Order of King Fred.

"At once, Your Majesty," the advisor vowed as he bowed and backed out of the room.

King Fred finished his porridge and began his morning wash-up. Every day, he bathed in the royal tub, shaved his royal chin, and waxed his royal mustache.

He had just risen from his bath and was busy lathering his face when the advisor once again burst into the room. This interruption had a jarring effect upon the royal reflexes. King Fred's hand knocked over his shaving mirror, causing it to smash on the bathroom floor.

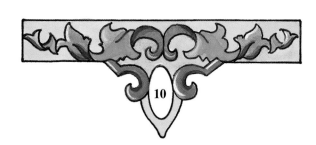

"Oh no, Your Majesty! This is total ruin! Breaking a mirror dooms you to seven years of bad luck!" the advisor cried.

"Seven years!" King Fred gulped. "Drat! The bad luck I got from spilling the salt has now stretched into seven years. Oh dear, oh dear, oh dear."

He sat down on the side of the bathtub and shook his head. "We must protect my people from such a fate. Make another royal proclamation that from now on, all mirrors are banished from the kingdom."

"At once, Your Majesty," the advisor vowed as he bowed and backed out of the room.

King Fred was now very sad and worried, and he took no delight in dressing in his favorite blue uniform. He even forgot to wax his mustache, which was drooping slightly at the ends. Before his unlucky morning, he'd really been looking forward to visiting the kingdom's new mill.

Now, however, he found his steps dragging as he approached the royal coach.

"Oh no, Your Majesty!" cried the advisor as he scrambled down the steps. "If you step on a crack, you break your mother's back!"

King Fred looked down at his feet. He was indeed stepping on a crack. Hoping to save his mother's back, he jumped off the crack as quickly as he could.

Then he thought of all the other mothers in his kingdom whose backs could be broken so easily by thoughtless children.

"It's time for another royal proclamation. From now on, all roads are to be torn up so there will be no more cracks that can break mothers' backs," King Fred announced wearily.

"At once, Your Majesty," the advisor vowed.

Hear Ye!
Hear Ye!

Let it be known that from this day forward, cracks in the road are banished from the kingdom by Royal Order of King Fred.

"And now I shall return to my room and spend the rest of the day in bed before I do any more harm to myself or my subjects with all of this bad luck."

"As you wish, Your Majesty," the advisor vowed as the king went back up the steps and entered the palace.

CHAPTER 2

The next morning, King Fred was miserable.

The night before, a violent thunderstorm had raged for hours and hours, shaking the palace walls and pounding the palace roof.

Even worse, his bed was full of the salt he had thrown over his shoulder. No matter how much he brushed off the sheets, there was still enough left to scratch his skin.

He heard a tapping at the door. It was the royal gardener. After hearing of the king's woes, she had brought King Fred another four-leaf clover because three such clovers are always better than two. King Fred was very relieved. Surely the new clover would break his run of bad luck.

He felt a little better when the servant arrived with his breakfast tray. King Fred dug the spoon into his favorite porridge and scooped up a mouthful. The hot cereal rolled over his tongue and down his throat.

He started to smack his lips, then he paused. Something was not quite right. He took a smaller spoonful and tried the porridge again. There was no flavor. The porridge tasted like warm paste.

The king pushed the tray aside and called for the royal cook. Within minutes, the cook shuffled through the door, wringing his hands in his apron and bobbing his head up and down.

King Fred said, "Something is very wrong. My porridge tastes like paste."

"I'm sorry, Your Majesty. I made it the same way I always do, but I didn't add salt, because yesterday you forbade the use of it."

"Humph. You mean salt made the difference?" When the cook nervously nodded, King Fred said, "Well, it's time for a change anyway. From now on, I'll just have something very simple for breakfast like... toast."

The cook bowed and backed out of the room, saying, "As you please, Your Majesty. Your wish is always my command, Your Majesty."

King Fred threw back the covers and went into the bathroom. His bath did much to restore his humor, but after he lathered his face, he found it very difficult to shave without a mirror.

In fact, he nicked himself thirteen times. And it was almost impossible to twist his mustache into the proper curl without a mirror. All he could manage was a lopsided spiral.

King Fred slowly perked up again as he dressed in his second-favorite green uniform and went to his coach to go on the postponed mill visit.

He hadn't gone very far when the coach squelched to a stop. He rapped on the ceiling and called to his driver.

"What is it you wish, Your Majesty?" his driver replied.

"Why have we stopped?" King Fred asked grumpily.

"Well, Your Majesty, all the roads have been torn up to get rid of any cracks, and there is only dirt left for a surface. The storm last night didn't help much either. So, as you can see, we are firmly stuck in the mud."

No matter which way the horses heaved, the coach barely moved. They were indeed stuck. King Fred completely ruined his second-favorite uniform and boots walking through the sloppy, muddy muck back to the palace.

CHAPTER 3

When the droopy-mustached, muddy, grumpy king entered the Grand Hall, a black cat leaped down from a windowsill and padded over to meet him.

"Oh no, Your Majesty!" the advisor cried. "A black cat crossing your path is the worst of bad luck. You must get rid of it immediately."

"*What?* Get rid of Snookums?"

"Of course, Your Majesty! You'll never have good luck if you don't!"

King Fred then stroked his chin and thought about the past day. He winced slightly when his fingers touched one of his shaving nicks. He remembered the tasteless porridge, and he looked down at his ruined uniform, which had always been his second-favorite one.

"I think it is time for another proclamation. From now on, the royal advisor will be banished from the kingdom."

"At once, Your Maj..., I mean, Your Majesty! I cannot banish myself," the advisor said.

"No, but *I* can. I'm happy to say your presence is no longer required in this kingdom."

"But, Your Majesty, I only advised you for your own good."

"You had me get rid of salt, mirrors, and roads, and now you say you want me to get rid of Snookums. She comes from a long line of mousers. Besides, she's my kitty cat. Now be gone! And never darken our doorstep again."

The guards dragged out the not-so-royal advisor, who cried, "Oh no!"

Smiling, King Fred bent down and picked up his cat.

"He was a very bad advisor, Snookums. I simply can't have him spreading his ideas all over my kingdom. After all, people make their own good luck."

Snookums seemed to agree, for her purring grew louder and louder.

King Fred reversed all of the previous day's proclamations.

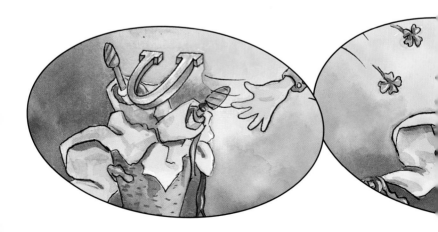

He threw away his horseshoe and the three four-leaf clovers, and put the lucky penny in his piggy bank.

Best of all, he never again let superstitions rule his life, although he still said "gesundheit" whenever somebody sneezed. After all, it was the polite thing to do.

THE SUPERSTITIONS OF KING FRED

Many of the superstitions that King Fred believed in are actually hundreds of years old.

Opening an Umbrella

In the past, people used umbrellas as protection from the sun. Long ago in parts of Asia, opening an umbrella in the shade, and especially in the house, was considered an insult to the power of the sun and brought bad luck.

Finding a Four-Leaf Clover

Most clovers grow with three leaves to a stem. From time to time, a clover with four leaves will grow. Because this doesn't happen very often, a person who finds a four-leaf clover is considered lucky.

Walking under a Ladder

Walking under a ladder is considered bad luck because paint or tools might fall on you. It is also bad luck because you might cause the person on the ladder to fall off. Long ago in England, condemned prisoners were forced to walk under the gallows ladder before they were hanged. Now that *is* bad luck!

Saying "Gesundheit"

Everyone knows that when a person gets a cold, they sneeze a lot. In the past, people believed sneezing was a sign of serious illness. That is why it became customary to say things like "gesundheit" or "salud" – which mean "good health to you" – to protect the person from the bad luck of getting sick.

Breaking a Mirror

Breaking a mirror is thought to be bad luck because long ago many people believed that if you looked into a mirror, you could see your future. If you broke that mirror, your future would be broken, too.

Seeing a Black Cat

Over the years, many people have been scared of things "that go bump in the night." Black cats, which can creep through the night unseen and unheard, were considered bad luck, especially if they crossed your path.

From the Author and Illustrator

When I was little, my father read us Irish folktales and stories about Robin Hood. As I grew older, I made up my own bedtime stories before falling asleep. I still tell myself stories, but now someone pays me to write them down. Talk about dreams coming true!

Anna-Maria Crum

ALL THE WORLD'S A STAGE

All the World's a Stage!
Which Way, Jack?
The Bad Luck of King Fred
Famous Animals
Puppets
The Wish Fish

WILD AND WONDERFUL

Winter Survival
Peter the Pumpkin-Eater
Because of Walter
Humphrey
Hairy Little Critters
The Story of Small Fry

FRIENDS AND FRIENDSHIP

Uncle Tease
PS I Love You, Gramps
Friendship in Action
Midnight Rescue
Nightmare
You Can Canoe!

ACTION AND ADVENTURE

Dinosaur Girl
Amelia Earhart
Taking to the Air
No Trouble at All!
River Runners
The Midnight Pig

Written by **Anna-Maria Crum**
Illustrated by **Anna-Maria Crum**
Edited by **Rebecca McEwen**
Designed by **Pat Madorin**

02 01 00
10 9 8 7 6 5 4 3 2

Distributed in the United States by
Rigby
a division of Reed Elsevier Inc.
P.O. Box 797
Crystal Lake, IL 60039-0797

Printed by Colorcraft, Hong Kong
ISBN: 1-57257-730-4